Duck, Duck, Goose

by **Wiley Blevins**

illustrated by **Elliot Kreloff**

mhreadingwonders.com

©2016 Red Chair Press LLC. All rights reserved. Used with permission.

No part of this publication may be reproduced or distributed
in any form or by an means, or stored in a database or retrieval system, without
the prior written consent of McGraw-Hill Education, including, but not limited to,
network storage or transmission, or broadcast for distance learning.

Send all inquiries to:
McGraw-Hill Education
Two Penn Plaza
New York NY 10121

ISBN: 978-0-07-678373-1
MHID: 0-07-678373-1

Printed in China

10 11 12 13 14 DSS 29 28 27 26 25

Mimi hops on the bus.
Where is she going? The farm.
What will she see there?
Let's find out.

Lamb.

Hurry up, Lamb!
You don't want to be late.

Mimi thinks about the line of animals. "They must be giving out something good," she says to her friend.

Mimi skips to the pond.
There she sees some feathery friends.

Goose.
Oh no! The goose is on the loose.

"I'll catch it," yells Mimi.

Mimi chases the goose into the barn.
The animals are chatting away.

Moo. Moo. Cluck. Cackle. Hee-Haw!
Moo. Moo. Cluck. Cackle. . . .

Mimi giggles at the animals popping up in the mud.
Pig. Pig. Frog. Frog. Frog.

"Which animal will pop up next?" wonders Mimi.
Pig. Pig. Frog. Frog. Frog.
Pig. Pig. . . .

Goat?
How did that get in there?

Mimi smiles. "It's been a fun day at the farm. But now it's time to go home."

Mimi walks to the bus and hops on board to join her friends.

And the wheels on the bus go up and down,
round and round,

up and down, round and round,
as Mimi goes . . .

to sleep.